More Bach Around the Christmas Tree

arranged by Carol Klose

CONTENTS

Cherry Lane Music Company
Director of Publications/Project Editor: Mark Phillips

ISBN 978-1-57560-820-4

Visit our website at www.cherrylane.com

Bring a Torch, Jeannette Isabella

In the style of Jean-Phillippe Rameau

17th Century French Provençal Carol

Carol of the Bells

In the style of Franz Josef Haydn

Ukrainian Christmas Carol

4

Children Go Where I Send Thee

In the style of Scott Joplin

Traditional Spiritual

*Play eighth notes straight (no "Swing" feel)

D.S. al Coda

Coda

7

Coventry Carol

In the style of Henry Purcell

Traditional English Melody

Largo

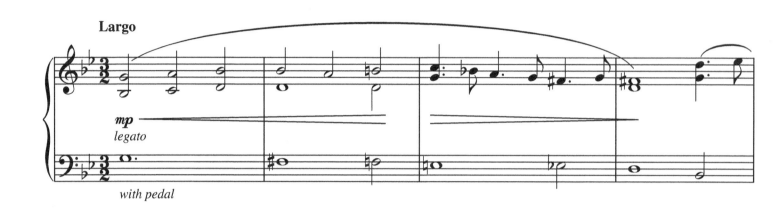

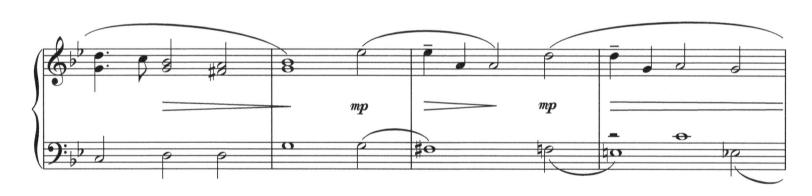

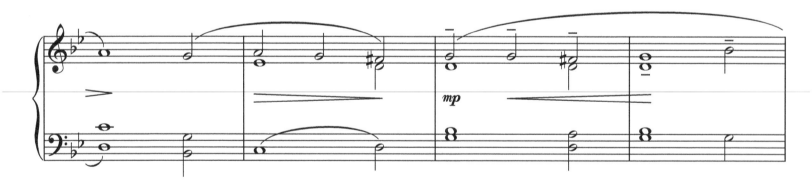

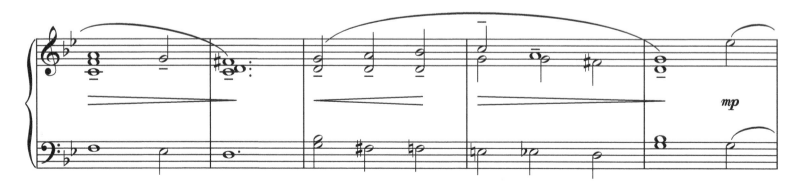

Ding Dong! Merrily on High!

In the style of Jean-Joseph Mouret

French Carol

Steady moderate tempo

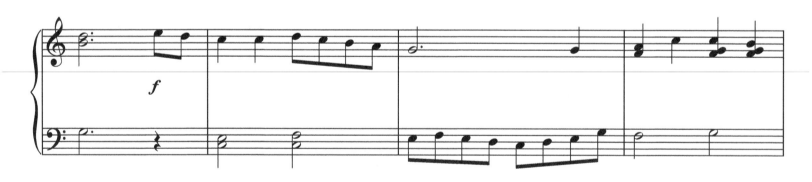

Gesù Bambino
In the style of Ludwig van Beethoven

Music by Pietro Yon

O Come, O Come, Emmanuel

In the style of Enrique Granados

Plainsong, 13th Century

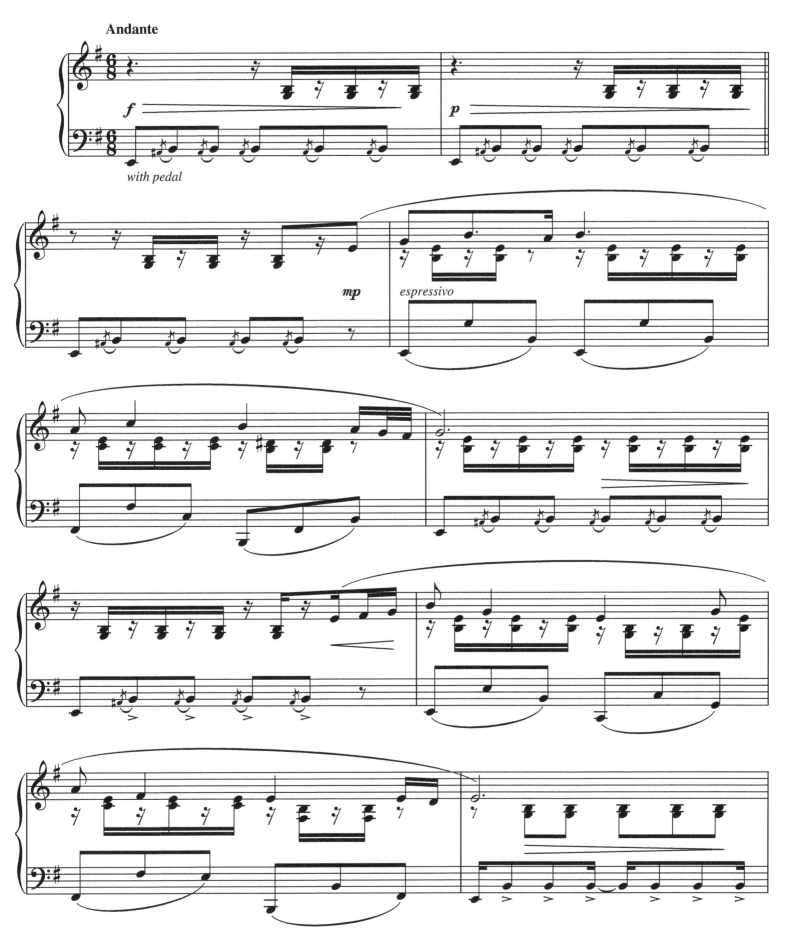

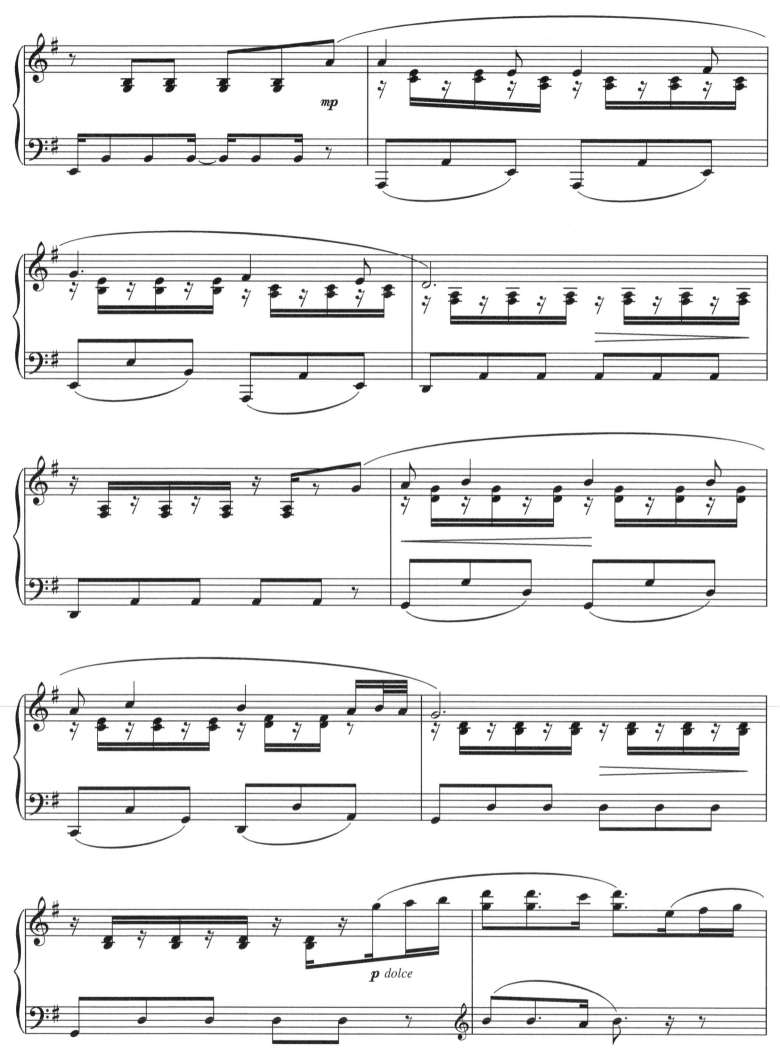

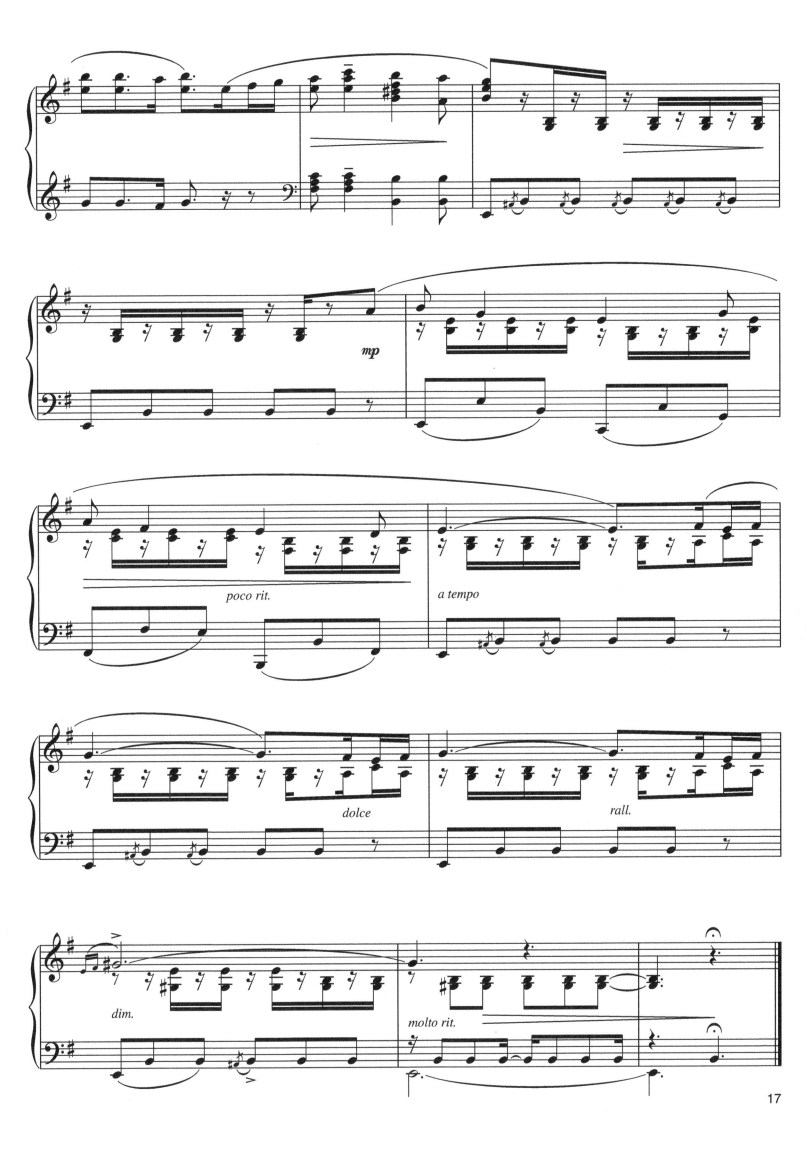

mp

poco rit.

a tempo

dolce

rall.

dim.

molto rit.

The Holly and the Ivy

In the style of J. Friedrich Burgmüller

18th Century English Carol

Moderately fast and flowing

I Saw Three Ships

In the style of Johann Sebastian Bach

Traditional English Carol

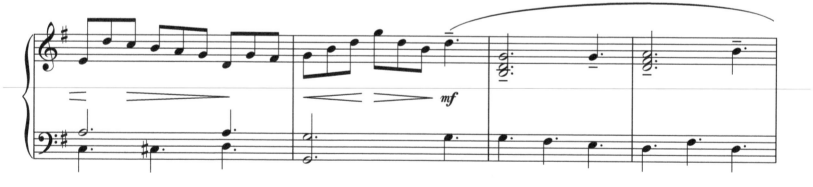

Pat-a-Pan

In the style of Peter Ilyitch Tchaikovsky

Music by Bernard de la Monnoye

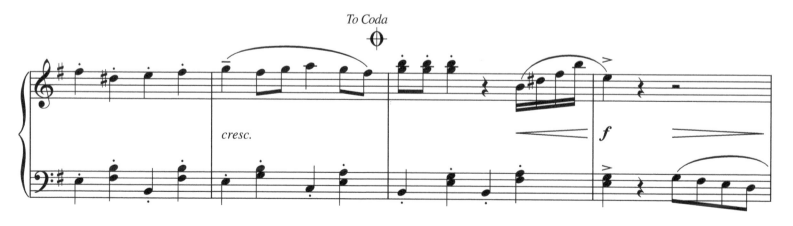

D.S. al Coda

Coda

23

Still, Still, Still

In the style of Wolfgang Amadeus Mozart

19th Century Salzburg Melody

Sussex Carol
In the style of Erik Satie

Traditional English Carol

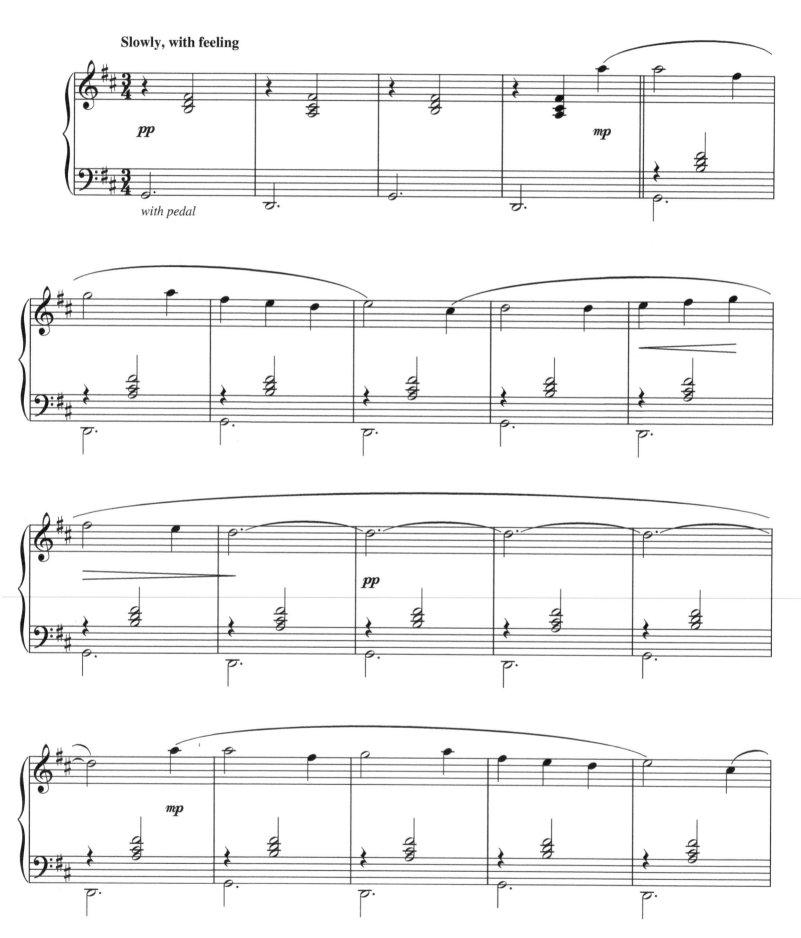

The Twelve Days of Christmas

In the style of Franz Liszt

Traditional English Carol

Creative PIANO SOLO

Looking to add some variety to your playing? Enjoy these beautifully distinctive arrangements for piano solo! These popular tunes get new and unique treatments for a fun and fresh presentation. Explore new styles and enjoy these favorites with a bit of a twist! Each collection includes 20 songs for the intermediate to advanced player.

BOHEMIAN RHAPSODY & OTHER EPIC SONGS

Band on the Run • A Day in the Life • Free Bird • November Rain • Piano Man • Roundabout • Stairway to Heaven • Take the Long Way Home • and more.

00196019 Piano Solo...$14.99

CHRISTMAS CAROLS

Away in a Manger • Deck the Hall • The First Noel • God Rest Ye Merry, Gentlemen • Hark! the Herald Angels Sing • It Came upon the Midnight Clear • Jingle Bells • Joy to the World • O Holy Night • Silent Night • Up on the Housetop • We Three Kings of Orient Are • What Child Is This? • and more.

00147214 Piano Solo...$14.99

CHRISTMAS COLLECTION

Blue Christmas • The Christmas Song (Chestnuts Roasting on an Open Fire) • Frosty the Snow Man • Here Comes Santa Claus (Right down Santa Claus Lane) • Let It Snow! Let It Snow! Let It Snow! • Silver Bells • Sleigh Ride • White Christmas • Winter Wonderland • and more.

00172042 Piano Solo...$14.99

CLASSIC ROCK

Another One Bites the Dust • Aqualung • Beast of Burden • Born to Be Wild • Carry on Wayward Son • Layla • Owner of a Lonely Heart • Roxanne • Smoke on the Water • Sweet Emotion • Takin' It to the Streets • 25 or 6 to 4 • Welcome to the Jungle • and more!

00138517 Piano Solo...$14.99

Prices, contents, and availability subject to change without notice.

DISNEY FAVORITES

Beauty and the Beast • Can You Feel the Love Tonight • Chim Chim Cher-ee • For the First Time in Forever • How Far I'll Go • Let It Go • Mickey Mouse March • Remember Me (Ernesto de la Cruz) • You'll Be in My Heart • You've Got a Friend in Me • and more.

00283318 Piano Solo...$14.99

JAZZ POP SONGS

Don't Know Why • I Just Called to Say I Love You • I Put a Spell on You • Just the Way You Are • Killing Me Softly with His Song • Mack the Knife • Michelle • Smooth Operator • Sunny • Take Five • What a Wonderful World • and more.

00195426 Piano Solo...$14.99

JAZZ STANDARDS

All the Things You Are • Beyond the Sea • Georgia on My Mind • In the Wee Small Hours of the Morning • The Lady Is a Tramp • Like Someone in Love • A Nightingale Sang in Berkeley Square • Someone to Watch Over Me • That's All • What'll I Do? • and more.

00283317 Piano Solo...$14.99

POP BALLADS

Against All Odds (Take a Look at Me Now) • Bridge over Troubled Water • Fields of Gold • Hello • I Want to Know What Love Is • Imagine • In Your Eyes • Let It Be • She's Got a Way • Total Eclipse of the Heart • You Are So Beautiful • Your Song • and more.

00195425 Piano Solo...$14.99

POP HITS

Billie Jean • Fields of Gold • Get Lucky • Happy • Ho Hey • I'm Yours • Just the Way You Are • Let It Go • Poker Face • Radioactive • Roar • Rolling in the Deep • Royals • Smells like Teen Spirit • Viva la Vida • Wonderwall • and more.

00138156 Piano Solo...$14.99

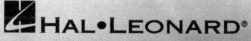

HAL•LEONARD®

www.halleonard.com

Looking to add some variety to your playing? Enjoy these beautifully distinctive arrangements for piano solo! These popular tunes get new and unique treatments for a fun and fresh presentation. Explore new styles and enjoy these favorites with a bit of a twist! Each collection includes 20 songs for the intermediate to advanced player.

CHRISTMAS CAROLS

Away in a Manger • Deck the Hall • The First Noel • God Rest Ye Merry, Gentlemen • Hark! the Herald Angels Sing • It Came upon the Midnight Clear • Jingle Bells • Joy to the World • O Holy Night • Silent Night • Up on the Housetop • We Three Kings of Orient Are • What Child Is This? • and more.

00147214 Piano Solo $14.99

CHRISTMAS COLLECTION

Blue Christmas • The Christmas Song (Chestnuts Roasting on an Open Fire) • Frosty the Snow Man • Here Comes Santa Claus (Right down Santa Claus Lane) • Let It Snow! Let It Snow! Let It Snow! • Silver Bells • Sleigh Ride • White Christmas • Winter Wonderland • and more.

00172042 Piano Solo $14.99

CLASSIC ROCK

Another One Bites the Dust • Aqualung • Beast of Burden • Born to Be Wild • Carry on Wayward Son • Layla • Owner of a Lonely Heart • Roxanne • Smoke on the Water • Sweet Emotion • Takin' It to the Streets • 25 or 6 to 4 • Welcome to the Jungle • and more!

00138517 Piano Solo $14.99

JAZZ POP SONGS

Don't Know Why • I Just Called to Say I Love You • I Put a Spell on You • Just the Way You Are • Killing Me Softly with His Song • Mack the Knife • Michelle • Smooth Operator • Sunny • Take Five • What a Wonderful World • and more.

00195426 Piano Solo $14.99

POP BALLADS

Against All Odds (Take a Look at Me Now) • Bridge over Troubled Water • Fields of Gold • Hello • I Want to Know What Love Is • Imagine • In Your Eyes • Let It Be • She's Got a Way • Total Eclipse of the Heart • You Are So Beautiful • Your Song • and more.

00195425 Piano Solo $14.99

POP HITS

Billie Jean • Fields of Gold • Get Lucky • Happy • Ho Hey • I'm Yours • Just the Way You Are • Let It Go • Poker Face • Radioactive • Roar • Rolling in the Deep • Royals • Smells like Teen Spirit • Viva la Vida • Wonderwall • and more.

00138156 Piano Solo $14.99

Prices, contents, and availability subject to change without notice.

HAL•LEONARD®
www.halleonard.com